The Whimsical Garden Gnomes
A Coloring Book For Adults

a
Chroma Tome
by
J.B. Johnson

Special Thanks To Our Fans
For Their Contributions To
This Chroma Tome!

Spyro Lee: Bee Gnome on page 7
Barbara Roberts: Gnome & Turtle on page 17
Traci Kelly: Hippie Gnome on page 45

Copyright   2016 J.B. Johnson
All rights reserved.
ISBN: - 1523788046
ISBN-13: 978-1523788040

Also Available from
CHROMA TOMES
and J.B. Johnson!

CHROMA TOMES

To learn more about Chroma Tomes' current line of
coloring books as well as all the news on
upcoming titles,
great contests,
and, of course, free stuff,
please visit us online at...

www.chromatomes.com
www.facebook.com/ChromaTomes
www.twitter.com/chromatomes

And remember, the Chroma Tomes team always loves to hear from you.
Color a Chroma Tomes picture, then either scan it, or take a clear photo of
it and send it to us via one of the options listed above and we will post it in
the online Chroma Tomes gallery!

A note to you from the CHROMA TOMES Crew

Thank you for supporting Chroma Tomes.
We value your feedback and always appreciate hearing
from you in order to continue to provide you with the best coloring
experience possible.

We also hope that you will take a moment to review your
Chroma Tome purchase on Amazon. com. Amazon reviews
are one of the best ways to support us. It means so much.

Thank you again for being a part of our Chroma Tome family.

Made in the USA
San Bernardino, CA
06 December 2016